TEST-TAKING SKILLS

GRADE 6

Y0-AEV-984

Written by
Jean Bunnell

Illustrated by
Mike Denman

Cover Illustration by
Barbara Friedman

Edited by
Barbara G. Hoffman

FS30206 Test-Taking Skills Grade 6
All rights reserved—Printed in the U.S.A.
Copyright © 1998 Frank Schaffer Publications, Inc.
23740 Hawthorne Blvd., Torrance, CA 90505

TEST-TAKING SKILLS
GRADE 6

Who likes tests? Not many people! A test puts us on the spot. Will we know the right answer? Will we remember the information being tested? Yet, most of us can learn how to prepare for a test, and how to test well.

This book looks at two different kinds of tests—classroom tests and standardized tests. Classroom tests usually require students to show what they know about a specific area of information, such as the concepts explained in a chapter of their science textbook, or the characters and plot of a short story or novel. There are almost always materials that can be studied to prepare for these tests. Standardized tests are different. They test what students know about a wide range of subjects. There are no specific materials students can review in order to study for them. Still, students can develop some strategies to help them do their very best when taking classroom and standardized tests.

This book begins with some questions to get students thinking about tests they've taken in the past. They develop techniques to help them study for classroom tests, including writing a test for someone else to take. They review strategies to manage their test-taking time, and to reduce their feelings of stress. They explore strategies for taking a variety of tests, including true/false, multiple choice, matching, and essay tests. Finally, students will be able to practice taking standardized tests in language arts and mathematics.

Key to icons:

 Time Management

 Planning

 Strategy

Practice

Name _____

Drawing on Experience

Think about the number of years you have been in school. During those years, you have probably taken many tests.

Answer the questions on this page about the last test you took.

1. The last test I took was about _____

_____

2. This is what I did to prepare for the test: (You may check more than one activity.)

_____completed homework as assigned

_____participated in classroom discussions

_____asked questions in or after class when I did not understand the material

_____got extra help on difficult material from the teacher, friend, or peer tutor

_____reviewed the material before the test

_____got enough sleep the night before the test

_____came to class with pencils, pens, or other items needed for the test

3. Before the test, I felt _____

_____

_____

4. After the test, I felt _____

_____

5. One thing I could do to improve my performance on tests is _____

_____

_____

6. Talk with a partner about taking tests. Share your answers to the questions on this page. Discover what your partner does to get ready for a test.

Name _____

Study Choices

To get the greatest benefit from test-taking strategies, you must be well-prepared. To prepare, you must thoroughly study and understand the material on which you are being tested.

There are a variety of study techniques. Several are listed below. These study techniques can be used for almost any subject.

Beside each technique, write at least two subjects for which this technique could be used. The first subject box is filled in for you.

Technique	Subject(s)
1. Make flash cards to memorize words, phrases, or facts.	*History* *Math*
2. Make up a "practice test" including questions you think might be asked on the test.	
3. Make an outline of the information in the textbook pages to be covered on the test.	
4. Read the notes you have taken in class.	
5. Study with a friend by asking each other questions about the material.	

Use Your Textbook!

One of the most important study tools you will ever use is one of the most obvious—your textbook! You can turn your textbook into your greatest ally when you are studying for a test.

- Get to know the format of your textbook. Besides reading the pages your teacher assigns in class, take the time to understand how your textbook is made up.

- Before your study session, consult your textbook and use the following exercise to help you study for any test.

Choose a chapter from your social studies book to review.

Write the name of the chapter. _____

Read the introduction. Write three sentences in your own words that tell what the chapter is about.

_____

_____

_____

Write two words that are printed in **boldface** or *italics*. Write definitions for each word.

_____

_____

_____

Look for graphic aids such as charts, graphs, maps, and captions to illustrations. Write two sentences describing one graphic aid.

_____

_____

_____

Read the summary section. Write three sentences in your own words telling what you have read in this chapter.

_____

_____

_____

Name _____

Write a Test

You have had years of experience taking tests, but you may not have had the chance to write and give a test. That is going to change! Giving a test will help you think about tests in a new way.

Test the arithmetic skills of a classmate. Get a blank piece of paper. Fold it into quarters. Number each section from 1 to 4. Print neatly so that your classmate will be able to read the exam.

A. In section 1, write addition and subtraction problems. Write one example problem, complete with a correct answer.

B. In section 2, write multiplication problems. Write one example problem, complete with a correct answer.

C. In section 3, write division problems. Write one example problem, complete with a correct answer.

D. In section 4, write a math word problem that can be solved through addition, subtraction, multiplication, or division.

E. Use the back of this paper to record the answers to the test you have written.

Exchange tests with a partner. Take the test your partner wrote while he or she takes the test you wrote. Set a time limit for completing the tests. Use the answer sheet you created to grade your partner's work on the test you wrote.

Teacher/Parent: After the students have completed the activity, encourage them to discuss their experiences writing an exam. What items were their partners able to do? What items were difficult? Were their partners able to complete the test? How could the test have been improved? How did it feel to create an exam? Finally, ask the students to consider how it felt to be giving the test instead of taking it.

Getting Ready for Tests

When is your next test? What material will it cover? What do you review?
Use this form to help keep yourself organized. In each section, first write the name of a subject in which you have a test. Then fill in the rest of the information about an upcoming test.

Subject: _____	Subject: _____
Next test date: _____	Next test date: _____
Test will cover: _____	Test will cover: _____
_____	_____
Materials I need to review:_____	Materials I need to review:_____
textbook pages: _____	textbook pages: _____
class notes: _____	class notes: _____
hand outs: _____	hand outs: _____
related quizzes: _____	related quizzes: _____
I plan to study at these times: _____	I plan to study at these times: _____
_____	_____
Subject: _____	Subject: _____
Next test date: _____	Next test date: _____
Test will cover: _____	Test will cover: _____
_____	_____
Materials I need to review:_____	Materials I need to review:_____
textbook pages: _____	textbook pages: _____
class notes: _____	class notes: _____
hand outs: _____	hand outs: _____
related quizzes: _____	related quizzes: _____
I plan to study at these times: _____	I plan to study at these times: _____
_____	_____

    FS30206 Test-Taking Skills

Name _____

Use Your Time Wisely

- There is a limited time in which to complete all the items on a test. It is important to use your time well. Spending too much time on a difficult item may prevent you from getting to other items which you can answer easily. Learning how to budget your test time is a skill you can master.

- Start with this practice test. First, skim through the test to identify the questions you can easily answer. Circle these problems and complete them first. Then complete the harder problems. This leaves the more difficult problems for later and ensures that you don't spend **all** your time trying to answer them.

You have 15 minutes to complete the following 10-question practice test.

a.
$$80 \times 87$$

b.
$$6082 - 5987$$

c.
$$1.8 \overline{)32.076}$$

d.
$$22 \ 3/8 + 47 \ 3/4$$

e.
$$7\tfrac{3}{4} \times 5$$

f.
$$\begin{array}{r} 29 \\ 586 \\ 39 \\ 5 \\ + \ 697 \\ \hline \end{array}$$

g.
$$9 \ 7/8 - 6 \ 3/4$$

h.
$$25.98 \times 3.4$$

i.
$$\begin{array}{r} 89.72 \\ 78.93 \\ + \ 24.89 \\ \hline \end{array}$$

j.
$$.9 \overline{)7000}$$

....

Teacher/Parent: Review the importance of budgeting one's time carefully during a test. Distribute the practice test. Remind students that they have 15 minutes to complete the test. Urge them to move rapidly from problem to problem answering the easiest questions first, then returning to complete the more difficult ones. Signal the start of the 15-minute test period. Advise students when 5 minutes have passed and again when 10 minutes have passed. Stop the test at the end of 15 minutes.

Name_____

Making a Test Plan

It is important to budget your time wisely during a test to make sure you have enough time to answer all the items. Often, you can plan the use of your time by looking over a test as soon as you receive it and estimating the number of minutes you'll need to complete each section.

You will have 30 minutes to complete the following test. Before the time begins, look at the four sections of the test. Estimate the number of minutes you will need to complete each section and write the number in the space beside each section.

I.   *True/False*   *Time I plan to spend on this section:* _____

Write a **T** next to the true statements and an **F** next to the false statements.

_____ 1. The first U.S. flag had 13 stars, one for each person who wrote the Constitution.

_____ 2. Hawaii was the fiftieth state added to the United States.

_____ 3. Alaska is the northernmost state in the United States.

II. *Multiple Choice*   *Time I plan to spend on this section:* _____

Fill in the bubble next to each correct answer.

1. One state which borders the Atlantic Ocean is:
   ⓐ Florida   ⓑ Nevada   ⓒ Idaho

2. One state sharing a border with Canada is:
   ⓐ Texas   ⓑ Arizona   ⓒ Montana

3. One state which borders the Pacific Ocean is:
   ⓐ California   ⓑ Oklahoma   ⓒ Rhode Island

III. *Matching*   *Time I plan to spend on this section:* _____

Draw a line from each state capital to its answer on the right.

1. Sacramento   is the capital of Alabama

2. Columbus   is the capital of Ohio

3. Birmingham   is the capital of California

IV. *Essay*   *Time I plan to spend on this section:* _____

Write an essay titled "My town or city is a great place to live." Use scrap paper to write down notes about what you want to say. Provide at least three detailed reasons to support your opinion. Write your essay on another sheet of paper.

Name _____

Reducing Test Stress

Your emotions can help you or hurt you during a test, just like they can influence your performance in a sport or artistic activity. A feeling of anticipation can increase your alertness and improve your performance. Feeling too much stress, however, may distract you and hurt your test performance.

Answer the following questions, and plan a strategy for reducing stress at the time of your next test.

- Know when a test will be given.
- Make time to study for the test.
- Get plenty of rest before the test.
- Eat nutritious food to fuel your brain and body.

1. What is the date and subject of your next test? Be specific. Is it a science test on electricity? Is it a math test on multiplying fractions? Is it a reading test on a specific book?

   _____

2. What is your study plan? Be specific. What day (or days) and at what times will you study? What technique(s) will you use for your study?

   _____

   _____

   _____

3. To be alert and ready to do your best, it is important to be well rested.

   How many hours of sleep do you need each night to feel completely rested? _____

   To be fully rested, what time will you need to go to bed the night before the test? _____

4. For your body to do its best, you need to eat a healthy and balanced diet on test day. What will you have for breakfast on test day? If the test is in the afternoon, what will you have for lunch that day?

   _____

   _____

   _____

Name _____

Follow Directions!

One of the most important rules for taking tests is to read carefully and to follow directions. Look at the words in the box. They are some of the important key words that tell you what to do.

Check	Cross out	Write	Circle	Match	Select
Draw	Read	Choose	Underline	List	Connect

Read the directions below. Underline the key words that tell you what to do. Start by underlining the key words in these directions. Then follow the directions. Watch for directions that may have more than one key word.

1. List three North American explorers. _____

_____

_____

2. Read each sentence below. Circle a **T** if the sentence is true and an **F** is the sentence is false.

   a. The Mediterranean Sea is located south of North America.   **T**   **F**

   b. The Indian Ocean is located east of Africa.   **T**   **F**

   c. Canada borders the Hudson Bay.   **T**   **F**

3. Draw a line from each word on the left to its definition on the right.

   a. igloo   building made of sun-dried clay or clay bricks

   b. tepee   a house built of ice or hard snow

   c. adobe   a cone-shaped tent made of hides or bark

4. Choose one topic below and write three sentences about the topic.

     My Favorite Pet   A Vacation to Remember   What I Look for in a Friend

_____

_____

_____

_____

        FS30206 Test-Taking Skills

Eliminating Wrong Choices

Some tests ask a question and then give several possible answers. You are asked to choose the best answer for each question. These tests are called multiple choice.

Example: Fill in the circle for the best answer.

How many days are in one year?

ⓐ 367   ● 365   ⓒ 362   ⓓ 300

● Eliminate some answers. What if you don't *know* the correct answer? Will you automatically miss the question? Not necessarily. Use what you *do* know to eliminate some of the other answers.

Example 1: June is the month we celebrate _____ .

    ⓐ Christmas   ⓑ Flag Day   ⓒ Rosh Hashanah   ⓓ St. Patrick's Day

You may not know the answer, but you might know some choices that are wrong. Christmas is celebrated in _____ and St. Patrick's Day is celebrated in _____ .

That leaves two choices. What do you think we celebrate in June? _____ . Fill in the circle for the correct answer.

Now look at the next question.

Example 2: Around 100 AD, the Buddhist religion came to China from _____ .

    ⓐ India   ⓑ France   ⓒ the United States   ⓓ Spain

Around 100 AD, the *United States* did not exist. Therefore, the Buddhist religion could not have come from the United States. Are the French and Spanish known as predominately Buddhist today? From where do you think the Buddhist religion came to China?

Look at these problems. Draw a line through the answers you know are incorrect. Then look at the remaining possible answers and fill in the circle for the correct answer.

3. The word *tolerance* means _____ .
    ⓐ no alcohol allowed   ⓒ respect for differences
    ⓑ sign telling the amount of toll   ⓓ a kind of painting

4. The word *compromise* means _____ .
    ⓐ a promise that is not true   ⓒ a promise made by someone in jail
    ⓑ a requirement   ⓓ an agreement in which both sides give up something

Multiple Choices

Use the following test-taking strategies.

- Follow directions carefully.
- Eliminate some wrong choices.
- Determine the correct answer.

Complete the following multiple-choice test. Fill in the circle for the answer.

1. The only members of the animal kingdom that produce milk to feed their babies are called _____.

   ⓐ mammals ⓑ birds ⓒ reptiles ⓓ fish

2. Animals, such as kangaroos, that have pouches for carrying their babies are called _____.

   ⓐ amphibians ⓑ marsupials ⓒ vertebrates ⓓ people

3. The most advanced order of mammals includes monkeys, apes, and people. They are called _____.

   ⓐ rodents ⓑ primates ⓒ ungulates ⓓ hoofed animals

4. The animal listed below that is not a carnivore is _____.

   ⓐ cow ⓑ bear ⓒ seal ⓓ cat

5. An elephant can defend itself using its _____.

   ⓐ sharp claws ⓑ foul smell ⓒ tusks ⓓ whip-like tail

6. Over short distances, the fastest mammal is the _____.

   ⓐ cheetah ⓑ horse ⓒ buffalo ⓓ leopard

7. The largest mammal is the _____.

   ⓐ porpoise ⓑ giraffe ⓒ ape ⓓ blue whale.

8. Animals that keep the same body temperature when temperatures around them change are _____.

   ⓐ cold-blooded ⓑ fish ⓒ amphibious ⓓ warm-blooded

9. The only mammals that can fly are _____.

   ⓐ cats ⓑ bats ⓒ birds ⓓ owls

10. Scientists that study animals and animal life are called _____.

    ⓐ zoologists ⓑ archaeologists ⓒ anarchists ⓓ paleontologists

Name _____

Returning to Questions

Sometimes on tests there will be problems that seem to have several answers.

● Often, it is better to skip a difficult problem, complete the easier ones, and then return to the problems you skipped.

1. Some tests have items that need to be matched. Each item on the list to the left goes with one item on the list to the right.

   ice   shortcake

   strawberry   butter

   peanut   cream

These items are easy to match.

   Ice goes with _____.

   Strawberry goes with _____.

   Peanut goes with _____.

2. Sometimes the answers are not as easy to identify. Look at the lists below.

   ice   pie

   strawberry   butter

   peanut   shortcake

   pecan   cream

   Ice goes with _____.

   Strawberry goes with _____ and also with _____.

   Which one is the right answer? Skip strawberry for now.

   Peanut goes with _____.

   Pecan goes with _____.

   So what must be the correct match for strawberry? _____

3. **Draw a line from the month on the left to its matching description on the right.** One month could go with two descriptions. When you identify that month, skip it and match each of the other months with its descriptive phrase. Once the other months are matched, only one phrase will remain. Match the remaining phrase with the month that has two possible matches.

   June   We are thankful for our blessings.

   February   This begins with a day for practical jokes.

   November   This is a cold winter month.

   April   Sweethearts celebrate a day in this month.

   January   Summer begins.

Educated Guesses

Matching test may have one or more items that are unfamiliar to you.

- In a matching test, you can sometimes figure out the answer using information you **do** know about some of the items.

Look at this example. Draw a line from each item to its definition.

skew lines	lines that intersect to form right angles
parallel lines	lines in different planes that do not intersect
perpendicular lines	lines in the same plane that never intersect

You may not know what skew lines are, so skip it for now.

You probably know that parallel lines are _____.

and perpendicular lines are _____.

Now you can figure out that skew lines must be _____.

Below are two lists of famous people and their accomplishments. Write the letter of the person next to his or her matching accomplishment.

- First, match the people you do recognize with their accomplishments. Then, see if you can match people whose names are unfamiliar to you.

a. Louisa May Alcott	_____	16th president of the United States
b. Ludwig van Beethoven	_____	producer of animated cartoons
c. Walt Disney	_____	conductor on the Underground Railroad
d. Henry Ford	_____	author of *Tom Sawyer*
e. Abraham Lincoln	_____	author of *Little Women*
f. Harriet Tubman	_____	German composer
g. Sally Ride	_____	automobile manufacturer
h. Mark Twain	_____	first American woman in space

- Sometimes there are clues right in the items to be matched.

If you didn't know Walt Disney, you still might have recognized the name Disney and associated it with _____.

If you didn't know Henry Ford, you still might have recognized the name Ford and associated it with _____.

If you didn't know Ludwig van Beethoven, you still might have recognized the name Beethoven and associated it with _____.

Matching Test

Use the following test-taking strategies to help you on a matching test.

- Skip terms that seem to have several answers.

- Skip terms that aren't familiar to you.

- Return to the unfamiliar items after you have completed the easier ones. Try again to answer them.

Complete this matching test of geographic terms.

1. Write the letter of each geographic term next to its correct definition.

    a. desert   _____ low land between hills or mountains

    b. mesa   _____ bowl-shaped area of land surrounded by higher land

    c. prairie   _____ gap between mountains

    d. island   _____ raised mass of land smaller than a mountain

    e. basin   _____ body of land completely surrounded by water

    f. hill   _____ large, flat area of grassland with few or no trees

    g. mountain pass   _____ dry area of land where few plants grow

    h. valley   _____ wide, flat-topped mountain with steep sides

2. Write the letter of each geographical term next to its correct definition.

    a. ocean   _____ opening in the earth from which lava and gasses escape

    b. glacier   _____ large stream that runs into a larger body of water

    c. mountain   _____ body of water completely surrounded by land

    d. tree line   _____ sheltered body of water where ships can dock safely

    e. harbor   _____ steeply-raised land, much higher than nearby areas

    f. lake   _____ on a mountain, the area above which no trees grow

    g. river   _____ large ice mass that moves slowly over land

    h. volcano   _____ salty body of water that covers a large area of the earth

Looking for Key Words

On some tests, you may be asked to read a statement and then to decide if the statement is true or false. That decision may seem simple, but be careful! Just one little word can change a statement that seems true into one that is false, and vice-versa! Look at the following sentences.

A thermos bottle keeps liquid cold for several hours.

A thermos bottle always keeps liquid cold for several hours.

Is the first statement true or false? _____

Is the second statement true or false? _____

What word makes the two statements different?_____

- Some key words to watch in true/false tests are

always	never	every	all	none	only	no

When one of these words appears in a statement, the statement is *usually* false.

     a. All dogs have brown fur.

     b. Automobiles run only on gasoline.

     c. Baseball is a sport every child likes to play.

Look at the following statements and circle the word that makes each of these statements false. On the lines below, rewrite the statements so that they are true.

     a. _____

     b. _____

     c. _____

- Remember, though, that sentences with the key words listed above *are not always* false. Consider these statements:

The sun always shines.

All children are younger than their parents.

Write a sentence that uses one of these key words, but is still true.

_____

_____

Name _____

Find the Truth

Read each statement. Decide if the statement is true or false. Look for key words like *always, never, every, all, none, only,* and *no* to help you decide. Circle these key words. Then, if the statement is true, write a T on the line. If the statement is false, write an F on the line.

_____ 1. The writers of the Declaration of Independence were always in full agreement.

_____ 2. The 4th of July is never on Sunday.

_____ 3. There are 12 inches in a foot, and 1 foot equals 3 yards.

_____ 4. One dollar is equal to twenty dimes.

_____ 5. Distance is always measured in miles.

_____ 6. A pint is always larger than a cup and smaller than a gallon.

_____ 7. October is the eighth month of the year.

_____ 8. It never rains in the United States in the summer.

_____ 9. All triangles have three sides and three angles.

_____10. Thirty-two days equals four weeks and four days.

_____11. Frozen water is usually called ice.

_____12. Two hours and thirteen minutes is equal to two hundred thirteen minutes.

_____13. Every man wants to play baseball.

_____14. Most children in the United States are immunized against polio.

_____15. Tornados never occur in the Middle Atlantic states.

FS30206 Test-Taking Skills

Organizing Your Ideas

Some tests include a question which you must answer in an essay. For some essays, you must write a persuasive argument defending your opinion on a specific topic. To write persuasively, you must organize your ideas before starting to write.

Read the essay question below.

A class of sixth graders recently wrote to the President of the United States. The students think sixth graders should be able to vote in the presidential election. If you were the president, how would you respond to their letter?

- Before starting to write, organize your ideas. Don't worry about using sentences or putting your thoughts in order.

First, use a few words to get your ideas on paper.

Why do you think the idea of sixth graders voting is a good idea?

_____

_____

_____

_____

Why do you think the idea of sixth graders voting is a bad idea?

_____

_____

_____

_____

After reviewing the good and bad, what is your opinion about sixth graders voting?

_____

_____

_____

_____

Now, think about the order in which you would include these ideas in your letter to the sixth-grade class. Ask yourself what order would make the most interesting and persuasive letter. Put a #1 next to the idea you would write about first, a #2 beside the next idea, etc.

Finally, write your letter on another piece of paper.

Name _____

Ordering Your Thoughts

There are many different ways to organize your ideas before starting to write an essay. Think about this essay topic:

Birthdays can be very special occasions. Think about one birthday celebration that was special for you. What made it so special?

- One way to organize your thoughts is to answer these questions: who? what? where? when? how? why?

Answering the questions below will help you plan out your answer to the essay. At first, don't worry about writing sentences or putting your thoughts in a strict order. Just use a few words to get your ideas on paper. Then, after you have written all your ideas, number them in the order you would use them in an essay.

Who was involved in your special birthday celebration?

_____

_____

What happened at the celebration and what did you think about it?

_____

_____

Where did it happen?

_____

_____

When did it happen?

_____

_____

How do you feel about the celebration now that some time has passed since it occurred?

_____

_____

Why do you remember it as such a special celebration?

_____

_____

Now, on another sheet of paper, write your essay.

Express Yourself!

Think of a sport, fine art, or other extra-curricular activity in which you are involved. Write an essay to persuade another sixth-grade student to become involved in the activity.

Begin your essay by jotting down several reasons why the student should participate in the activity. Use the space below for your notes. Then number your ideas according to the order in which you will discuss them in your essay.

_____

_____

_____

_____

_____

_____

_____

_____

_____

_____

_____

On a separate sheet of paper, write your essay. Include three paragraphs in your essay.

- The first paragraph is an introduction. It should tell the reader the main idea of your essay and how you are going to present the information.

- The second paragraph is the part of the essay in which you present points that support your main idea in a logical and interesting order.

- The third paragraph is the conclusion, in which you briefly review your main idea and the points that support it.

- Remember to write a topic sentence for each paragraph.

A Standardized Test Answer Sheet

Use this answer sheet for the standardized tests following this page.

Use only a #2 pencil. Write the title of the test you are taking at the top of the page. Fill in the answer circles as completely and darkly as possible. If you change your answer, be sure to completely erase your first choice. Do not make any marks on this page besides your answers and the section title.

Test: _____

1. ⓐ ⓑ ⓒ ⓓ

2. ⓐ ⓑ ⓒ ⓓ

3. ⓐ ⓑ ⓒ ⓓ

4. ⓐ ⓑ ⓒ ⓓ

5. ⓐ ⓑ ⓒ ⓓ

6. ⓐ ⓑ ⓒ ⓓ

7. ⓐ ⓑ ⓒ ⓓ

8. ⓐ ⓑ ⓒ ⓓ

9. ⓐ ⓑ ⓒ ⓓ

10. ⓐ ⓑ ⓒ ⓓ

11. ⓐ ⓑ ⓒ ⓓ

12. ⓐ ⓑ ⓒ ⓓ

Teacher/Parent: Give each student a copy of this page for each section of the standardized test. These tests are on pages 23-30 in this book. You can also use it in conjunction with tests you write yourself.

Reading a Fable

Reading comprehension tests assess your understanding of what you read.

- When you take a reading comprehension test, read the questions first.
  Then read the story or passage, and finally answer the questions.

The following story is one of Aesop's fables. Read the story and then answer the questions. Record your answers on the answer sheet. Allow 15 minutes for the test.

Once there was a thirsty crow. She had flown a long way and was looking for water to drink. Suddenly she saw a pitcher. She flew down and saw that it had a little water, but the water was so low in the pitcher that she could not reach it.

"But I must have that water!" she cried. "I am too weary to fly further. What shall I do? I know! I'll tip the pitcher over." She beat it with her wings, but it was too heavy. She could not move it.

Then she thought awhile. "Now I know! I will break the pitcher! Then I will drink the water as it pours out. How good it will taste!" With beak and claws and wings, she threw herself against the pitcher, but it was too strong.

The poor crow stopped to rest. "What shall I do now? I cannot die of thirst with water close by. There must be a way, if only I had wit enough to find it out."

After a while, the crow had a bright idea. There were many small stones lying about. She picked them up one by one and dropped them into the pitcher. Slowly the water rose until at last she could drink it. How good it tasted!

"There is always a way out of a hard place," said the crow, "if you have the wit to find it."

1. The writer of this fable is _____.
   (a) Longfellow   (b) Aesop   (c) Mr. Crow   (d) Mark Twain

2. The crow was thirsty because _____.
   (a) she was alone   (b) she had eaten fish   (c) it was hot   (d) she had flown a long way

3. The crow could not drink the water out of the pitcher because _____.
   (a) it was too cold   (b) the level was not high enough   (c) her wings were tired
   (d) she could not reach the pitcher

4. The crow did not tip the pitcher over because _____.
   (a) it would have broken   (b) it was too heavy   (c) it was too strong
   (d) it was tied to the table

5. The lesson taught in this fable is _____.
   (a) "Crows can think"   (b) "Use light-weight pitchers"   (c) "Small stones are best"
   (d) "Keep trying"

Read On

Reading comprehension tests assess your understanding of what you read.

- When you take a reading comprehension test, answer the easy questions first. Go back and check the passage to answer the others.

Read the passage below and then answer the questions. Record your answers on the answer sheet. Allow 15 minutes for the test.

Long before Europeans set foot on American soil, Navajos lived and thrived in America. Ancestors of the Navajo came from Alaska and northern Canada to live in the southwest of North America. Today, the Navajo are one of the largest groups of Native Americans in the United States. The Navajo Nation is located in Utah, Colorado, Arizona, and New Mexico. At 16 million acres, it is the largest reservation in the United States.

Navajo are farmers, sheepherders, weavers, and silversmiths. Since the 1600s, Navajo have farmed crops like corn and raised sheep, goats, and horses. From the wool of their sheep, the Navajo wove rugs, blankets, and clothing. Long ago, the Navajo also learned to make silver and turquoise jewelry. Today, some Navajo still farm and raise animals. Many are famous for their skills in weaving and jewelry-making.

Navajo are war veterans, miners, engineers, writers, lawyers, doctors, athletes, and artists. Others, like Annie Dodge Wauneka, have become important activists. She is a Navajo who has worked to improve the lives of her people in many ways. Navajos are important contributing members to life in the United States.

1. From this passage, what can you infer about the Navajo?
   ⓐ They migrated to the southwest of North America before the Pilgrims settled in New England.
   ⓑ They like to dance.
   ⓒ Today, Navajos are primarily engineers.
   ⓓ none of the above

2. The Navajo Nation is located on 16 million acres crossing the states of _____.
   ⓐ Utah, California, Nevada, and Colorado
   ⓑ Utah, Arizona, Colorado, and New Mexico
   ⓒ Utah, California, Colorado, and New Mexico
   ⓓ none of the above

3. The Navajos are farmers who raise animals like _____.
   ⓐ pigs, goats, and horses
   ⓑ cows, goats, and chickens
   ⓒ sheep, goats, and horses
   ⓓ none of the above

4. According to this passage, who is Annie Dodge Wauneka?
   ⓐ She is a weaver whose rugs and blankets are famous throughout the land.
   ⓑ She is the tribal leader of the Navajo Nation.
   ⓒ She is an important activist who has helped her people in many ways.
   ⓓ none of the above

5. According to the passage, the Navajo are famous for their skills as _____.
   ⓐ doctors and writers
   ⓑ artists and athletes
   ⓒ weavers and jewelry-makers
   ⓓ none of the above

6. What would be the best title for this passage?
   ⓐ "The Navajo: Native Americans"
   ⓑ "An Activist Named Annie Dodge Wauneka"
   ⓒ "A People in Crisis"
   ⓓ none of the above

Punctuation and Capitalization

In each of the items below, a sentence has been divided into three phrases. If you find a mistake in one of the three phrases, choose that phrase as your answer. If all the phrases in a sentence are correct, choose "no mistakes." Record your answers on the answer sheet. Allow 10 minutes for the test.

1.
   ⓐ Kelly Sullivan lives
   ⓑ at 27 green street
   ⓒ in Portland, Maine.
   ⓓ no mistakes

2.
   ⓐ Art likes, to go
   ⓑ hunting, fishing, and
   ⓒ hiking with his father.
   ⓓ no mistakes

3.
   ⓐ Robert frost wrote
   ⓑ a poem called
   ⓒ "The Road Not Taken."
   ⓓ no mistakes

4.
   ⓐ "Stop!" cried Adam.
   ⓑ "Come back here with
   ⓒ my bicycle."
   ⓓ no mistakes

5.
   ⓐ Anne Frank died
   ⓑ in a concentration camp
   ⓒ during world war II.
   ⓓ no mistakes

6.
   ⓐ "Will you go to
   ⓑ the movies with me?
   ⓒ asked Amy.
   ⓓ no mistakes

7.
   ⓐ On their trip, Joe's
   ⓑ family traveled to
   ⓒ washington dc and philadelphia.
   ⓓ no mistakes

8.
   ⓐ Mr and Mrs Arcuri
   ⓑ are pilots and are
   ⓒ teaching their children to fly.
   ⓓ no mistakes

9.
   ⓐ Will the basketball game
   ⓑ be played at Brown Academy
   ⓒ or at Memorial High.
   ⓓ no mistakes

10.
    ⓐ Math social studies and
    ⓑ science are three subjects
    ⓒ we study in school.
    ⓓ no mistakes

11.
    ⓐ "I like to read," Nora told Jody.
    ⓑ My favorite book is
    ⓒ *Little Women* by Louisa May Alcott."
    ⓓ no mistakes

12.
    ⓐ The supreme court of the
    ⓑ United States decides if laws
    ⓒ are constitutional or not.
    ⓓ no mistakes

25

Spell Check

One word is missing from each of the following sentences. Listed below each sentence are three different spellings of the missing word. Choose the word that is spelled correctly. If none of the choices are spelled correctly, choose "none of the above." Record your answers on the answer sheet. Allow 10 minutes for the test.

1. Fried _____ is my favorite food.
   - ⓐ chiken
   - ⓑ chicken
   - ⓒ chikkenn
   - ⓓ none of the above

2. Who is _____ for making this mess?
   - ⓐ responsible
   - ⓑ respondsable
   - ⓒ responsable
   - ⓓ none of the above

3. Feel the _____ on the cold glass.
   - ⓐ mousture
   - ⓑ moizture
   - ⓒ moisture
   - ⓓ none of the above

4. He has no _____ of that book.
   - ⓐ nowlege
   - ⓑ knowledge
   - ⓒ knolege
   - ⓓ none of the above

5. The English _____ is due today.
   - ⓐ composition
   - ⓑ conposishun
   - ⓒ compositian
   - ⓓ none of the above

6. The _____ is either 1/4 or 1/3.
   - ⓐ fracshun
   - ⓑ fraktion
   - ⓒ fractian
   - ⓓ none of the above

7. They did an _____ in science class.
   - ⓐ experiment
   - ⓑ experimant
   - ⓒ expearament
   - ⓓ none of the above

8. Maria plays games on her _____ .
   - ⓐ kompewter
   - ⓑ compooter
   - ⓒ computer
   - ⓓ none of the above

9. The game will start _____ .
   - ⓐ tomorrow
   - ⓑ tommorrow
   - ⓒ tomorow
   - ⓓ none of the above

10. That chair is more _____ than this one.
   - ⓐ comfortible
   - ⓑ comfortable
   - ⓒ kumfortable
   - ⓓ none of the above

11. The _____ is ringing.
   - ⓐ telefone
   - ⓑ teliphone
   - ⓒ tellaphon
   - ⓓ none of the above

12. The sunset _____ this song.
   - ⓐ enspired
   - ⓑ inspired
   - ⓒ innspirred
   - ⓓ none of the above

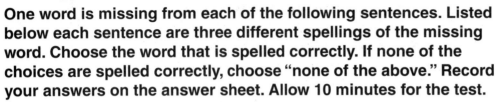

Name _____

What's the Definition?

One word is underlined in each of the following sentences. Choose the best definition for the word. If there is no satisfactory definition, choose "none of the above" as your answer. Record your answers on the answer sheet. Allow 10 minutes for the test.

1. A fence will <u>enclose</u> the garden.
   - (a) surround
   - (b) shut
   - (c) plant
   - (d) none of the above

2. The Town <u>Council</u> meets Tuesday.
   - (a) mayor
   - (b) governing body
   - (c) theater group
   - (d) none of the above

3. She had to <u>amuse</u> her little brother.
   - (a) entertain
   - (b) change
   - (c) hug
   - (d) none of the above

4. Teachers <u>encourage</u> us in our study.
   - (a) telephone
   - (b) force
   - (c) help
   - (d) none of the above

5. The president wrote an <u>autobiography</u>.
   - (a) speech about cars
   - (b) newspaper article
   - (c) song lyrics
   - (d) none of the above

6. Tom <u>witnessed</u> the accident.
   - (a) caused
   - (b) left
   - (c) saw
   - (d) none of the above

7. She is <u>unemployed</u> and has no money.
   - (a) underage
   - (b) without a job
   - (c) without job skills
   - (d) none of the above

8. The <u>discussion</u> was about politics.
   - (a) conversation
   - (b) meeting
   - (c) speech
   - (d) none of the above

9. She had <u>previous</u> singing experience.
   - (a) professional
   - (b) a large amount
   - (c) earlier
   - (d) none of the above

10. Please <u>describe</u> your costume.
    - (a) finish
    - (b) put on
    - (c) tell about
    - (d) none of the above

11. The pilot began the plane's <u>descent</u>.
    - (a) take-off
    - (b) instrument check
    - (c) radio contact
    - (d) none of the above

12. I <u>improvised</u> when I forgot my speech.
    - (a) made something up
    - (b) got embarrassed
    - (c) asked for a second chance
    - (d) none of the above

FS30206 Test-Taking Skills

Name _____

Figure It Out

Read each problem carefully. Find the answer for each problem and then record your answers on the answer sheet. You may use scrap paper. Allow 20 minutes for the test.

1. Round 2,876 to the nearest hundred.
   (a) 2,800
   (b) 3,000
   (c) 2,900
   (d) none of the above

2. What is a quadrilateral with exactly one pair of parallel sides?
   (a) square
   (b) rhombus
   (c) trapezoid
   (d) none of the above

3. Solve as an improper fraction. $3\frac{1}{2} =$
   (a) $\frac{7}{2}$
   (b) $\frac{6}{2}$
   (c) $\frac{8}{3}$
   (d) none of the above

4. $8\frac{3}{4} =$
   (a) 34
   (b) 8.75
   (c) 8.12
   (d) none of the above

5. $9 + (3 \times 2) =$
   (a) 14
   (b) 15
   (c) 24
   (d) none of the above

6. Find the area.

   16

   8 |_____| 8

   16
   (a) 46
   (b) 48
   (c) 50
   (d) none of the above

7. Each side of a pentagon is 5 inches long. What is the perimeter of the pentagon?
   (a) 3 feet, 1 inch
   (b) 50 inches
   (c) 5 feet, 5 inches
   (d) none of the above

8. Bob received the following grades on his math quizzes: 80, 74, 87, and 71. What is his average score?
   (a) 312
   (b) 78
   (c) 71
   (d) none of the above

9. What is $\frac{6}{20}$ in the lowest terms?
   (a) $\frac{3}{10}$
   (b) $\frac{4}{6}$
   (c) $\frac{12}{40}$
   (d) none of the above

10. Find the decimal for the following percent:
    38% =
    (a) 0.038
    (b) 0.38
    (c) 3.8
    (d) none of the above

11. Solve the proportion.
    $$\frac{5}{n} = \frac{20}{36}$$
    (a) 36
    (b) 7
    (c) 9
    (d) none of the above

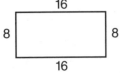

FS30206 Test-Taking Skills

Do the Math

Complete the following computations. You may use scrap paper.
Record your answers on the answer sheet. Allow 20 minutes for the test.

1. 26 + 302 + 800 =
   ⓐ 1,329
   ⓑ 1,362
   ⓒ 1,128
   ⓓ none of the above

2. 487 - 298 =
   ⓐ 271
   ⓑ 189
   ⓒ 239
   ⓓ none of the above

3. 492 x 18 =
   ⓐ 8,967
   ⓑ 7,892
   ⓒ 4,918
   ⓓ none of the above

4. 294 ÷ 14 =
   ⓐ 21
   ⓑ 23
   ⓒ 19
   ⓓ none of the above

5. 4.7 + 8.26 =
   ⓐ 12.96
   ⓑ 8.73
   ⓒ 12.267
   ⓓ none of the above

6. $8 - $4.56 =
   ⓐ $4.44
   ⓑ $4.56
   ⓒ $3.44
   ⓓ none of the above

7. 4 x 22.7 =
   ⓐ 9.08
   ⓑ 908
   ⓒ 90.8
   ⓓ none of the above

8. 23.42 x 8.6 =
   ⓐ 14.052
   ⓑ 201.412
   ⓒ 18.736
   ⓓ none of the above

9. 426 ÷ 18 =
   ⓐ 23.12
   ⓑ 23 2/3
   ⓒ 24 R3
   ⓓ none of the above

10. 48 ÷ 2.5 =
    ⓐ 20
    ⓑ 19.2
    ⓒ 18.6
    ⓓ none of the above

11. ¾ + ⅘ + ½ =
    ⓐ 2¹⁄₂₀
    ⓑ ⁸⁄₁₂
    ⓒ ⁸⁄₂₀
    ⓓ none of the above

12. 2¾ x 7½ =
    ⓐ 20⅝
    ⓑ 14⅜
    ⓒ 15
    ⓓ none of the above

FS30206 Test-Taking Skills

Find the Solution

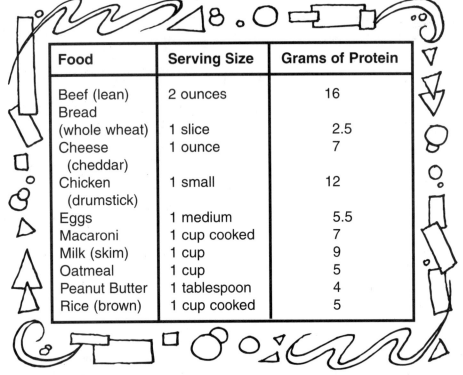

Food	Serving Size	Grams of Protein
Beef (lean)	2 ounces	16
Bread (whole wheat)	1 slice	2.5
Cheese (cheddar)	1 ounce	7
Chicken (drumstick)	1 small	12
Eggs	1 medium	5.5
Macaroni	1 cup cooked	7
Milk (skim)	1 cup	9
Oatmeal	1 cup	5
Peanut Butter	1 tablespoon	4
Rice (brown)	1 cup cooked	5

Use the information on this chart to solve the problems that follow. You may use scrap paper. Find the answer in the list below each problem. Record your answers on the answer sheet. Allow 20 minutes for this test.

1. How many cups of skim milk would Stacy have to drink to get 45 grams of protein?
   (a) 45 cups   (b) 5 cups   (c) 9 cups   (d) not given

2. George needs to eat about 70 grams of protein every day. For dinner he ate 4 chicken drumsticks. How many more grams does he need?
   (a) 22 grams   (b) 66 grams   (c) 58 grams   (d) not given

3. Soon-Yi had a cup of oatmeal with a cup of milk for breakfast, a sandwich with 2 slices of whole wheat bread, and 2 ounces of cheddar cheese for lunch. If she needs a total of 50 grams of protein each day, how many grams of protein should she have for dinner?
   (a) 23 grams   (b) 27 grams   (c) 8 grams   (d) not given

4. Mario wants to have approximately 20 grams of protein in his lunch. What should he eat?
   (a) a peanut butter sandwich (2 slices of bread and 2 tablespoons of peanut butter)
   (b) 2 chicken drumsticks and a cup of brown rice
   (c) macaroni and cheese (1 cup macaroni with 2 ounces of cheese)
   (d) not given

5. A pound of chicken has 144 grams of protein and will serve 4 people. How many grams of protein will each person get?
   (a) 48 grams   (b) 12 grams   (c) 36 grams   (d) not given

FS30206 Test-Taking Skills

Answers

Page 3
Answers will vary.

Page 4
Answers will vary.

Page 5
Answers will vary.

Page 6
Answers will vary.

Page 7
Answers will vary.

Page 8
a. 6960
b. 95
c. 17.82
d. 70 1/8
e. 38 3/4
f. 1356
g. 3 1/8
h. 88.332
i. 193.54
j. 7777.8

Page 9
I. 1. F
   2. T
   3. T
II. 1. a
   2. c
   3. a
III. 1. Sacramento, California
    2. Columbus, Ohio
    3. Birmingham, Alabama
IV. Answers will vary.

Page 10
Answers will vary.

Page 11
1. Answers will vary.
2. a. F
   b. T
   c. T
3. igloo=a house built of ice or hard snow
   tepee=a cone-shaped tent made of hides and bark
   adobe=building made of sun-dried clay or clay bricks
4. Answers will vary.

Page 12
1. b
   December, March, Flag Day
2. a
3. c
4. d

Page 13
1. a
2. b
3. b
4. a
5. c
6. a
7. d
8. d
9. b
10. a

Page 14
1. ice cream, strawberry shortcake, peanut butter
2. pecan pie
3. June=Summer begins.
   February=Sweethearts celebrate a day in this month.
   November=We are thankful for our blessings.
   April=This begins with a day for practical jokes.
   January=This is a cold winter month.

Page 15
Example:
parallel lines=lines on the same plane that never intersect
perpendicular lines=lines that intersect to form right angles
skew lines=lines on different planes that do not intersect
a. Alcott=author of Little Women
b. Beethoven=German composer
c. Disney=producer of animated cartoons
d. Ford=automobile manufacturer
e. Lincoln=16th president of the U.S.
f. Tubman=conductor on the Underground Railroad
g. Ride=first American woman in space
h. Twain=author of Tom Sawyer
cartoons, cars, music

Page 16
1. a. desert=dry area of land where few plants grow
   b. mesa=wide, flat-topped mountain with steep sides
   c. prairie=large, flat area of grassland with few or no trees
   d. island=body of land completely surrounded by water
   e. basin=bowl-shaped area of land surrounded by higher land
   f. hill=raised mass of land smaller than a mountain
   g. mountain pass=gap between mountains
   h. valley=low land between hills or mountains
2. a. ocean=salty body of water covering large areas of earth
   b. glacier=large ice mass that moves slowly over land
   c. mountain=steeply-raised land, much higher than nearby areas
   d. tree line=on a mountain, the area above which no trees grow
   e. harbor=sheltered body of water where ships can dock safely
   f. lake=body of water completely surrounded by land
   g. river=large stream that runs into a larger body of water
   h. volcano=opening in earth from which lava and gasses escape

Page 17
true, false, always
Circled words:
a. All; b. only; c. every
a. Some dogs have brown fur.
b. Some automobiles run on gasoline.
c. Baseball is a sport some children like to play.
Last answer will vary.

Answers

Page 18
1. F
2. F
3. F
4. F
5. F
6. T
7. F
8. F
9. T
10. T
11. T
12. F
13. F
14. T
15. F

Page 19
Answers will vary.

Page 20
Answers will vary.

Page 21
Answers will vary.

Page 23
1. b
2. d
3. b
4. b
5. d

Page 24
1. a
2. b
3. c
4. c
5. c
6. a

Page 25
1. b
2. a
3. a
4. d
5. c
6. b
7. c
8. a
9. c
10. a
11. b
12. a

Page 26
1. b
2. a
3. c
4. b
5. a
6. d
7. a
8. c
9. a
10. b
11. d
12. b

Page 27
1. a
2. b
3. a
4. c
5. d
6. c
7. b
8. a
9. c
10. c
11. d
12. a

Page 28
1. c
2. c
3. a
4. b
5. b
6. d
7. d
8. b
9. a
10. b
11. c

Page 29
1. c
2. b
3. d
4. a
5. a
6. c
7. c
8. b
9. b
10. b
11. a
12. a

Page 30
1. b
2. a
3. b
4. c
5. c

FS30206 Test-Taking Skills